Introduction
вступление

The most important step when learning a language is to be able to read the alphabet. You can also start learning Russian without the alphabet and you may even already know some Russian. The big disadvantage, however, is that without the alphabet you won't be able to read real Russian words, only the pronunciation of these words with the letters of our alphabet. But if you want to be able to read, write, understand and speak fluently, the smartest thing to do is to start directly with the alphabet and perfect it.

With languages such as Spanish, French or Italian, this step is not necessary. We can start learning vocabulary and grammar straight away, as they have exactly the same alphabet as us, apart from a few special characters. This is not the case with languages such as Arabic, Japanese or Russian. They use characters that are completely foreign to us, which we first have to learn.

The advantage of Russian is that its characters look very familiar to us. Some letters such as "A", for example, are even the same in Russian as they are here. At the same time, there are also letters like the Russian "H", which looks like our "H" but is pronounced [en], just like our "N". As this can quickly confuse beginners, you should pay particular attention to learning the letters accurately.

A notebook like this is perfect for memorizing the characters and learning to write beautifully. If we write things down again and again, they stay in our memory. In this book, you have 2 pages for each character to learn the letters in upper and lower case and then write them down again in the context of words. Every 5 letters there are also repetition exercises with words to go through all the letters you have learned so far. After the letters you will find further exercises to consolidate everything again. At the very end you will also find the 100 most important Russian vocabulary words, which you can cut out and use as flash cards.

I have also linked a learning app as an addition. You can use this to learn all the letters of the Russian Cyrillic alphabet and the words at the end of the book with digital flashcards. Follow the instructions 3 pages further on and get free access to the learning app.

If you work through this book from beginning to end and learn with the app, you will not only have learned the Russian alphabet, but perfected it.

The ideal learning plan

The alphabet is essential, but only the beginning. So that you are not lost once you have learned the alphabet, I have created a 4 step syllabus for anyone just starting to learn Russian.

The aim of these 4 steps is to reach A1 level, the first real level of Russian. The order of the steps is based on experience, which is 1. the fastest and 2. the most realistic for the learner. The main problem with any new language is motivation. If you don't have a syllabus and don't know how to learn properly, you will most likely stop after a few weeks and never learn the language properly. Having a plan, a goal and learning materials is therefore incredibly important to prevent yourself from giving up.

After you have worked through this book and mastered the alphabet (which should be the case in 1-2 weeks at the latest if you practise daily), the next step is to learn vocabulary.

Vocabulary is the most important part of any new language. Grammar and sentence structure are of course also extremely important, but nothing teaches you a language more effectively than simply learning vocabulary. A vocabulary of 500 words or more will give you such a good overview of any language that it will be much easier to persevere and learn all other aspects of a language.

That's why my second book is also a vocabulary book: "Your first 720 words in Russian" aims to teach you all 720 Russian A1 words in the most effective way and to give you a solid vocabulary. If you are interested, you can scan the QR code below or simply search for the title on Amazon.

www.amazon.com/dp/B0DNW913Y3

More information on this book

The Russian Learning Guide:

1

Learn the Russian Cyrillic alphabet

learn the Russian Cyrillic alphabet to be able to read
Russian texts. That's what this workbook is for.

2

Learn Your First 720 Russian Words

The A1 level in Russian corresponds to approximately 700 words. You will learn
these in my 2nd book and with the included learning app from the 2nd book.

3

Learn all the important rules of grammar

Understanding of the most important grammatical structures and
introduction of verbal aspects. I am currently working on a book about this.

4

Practicing conversations in everyday life

Together with the alphabet, vocabulary and grammar, you
can now practise simple conversations and really make use
of your new Russian language skills.

Quizlet access

In addition to this book, I have made all 33 letters and all 100 flashcards at the end of the book available to you for free via the Quizlet learning platform. So if you prefer to study with a smartphone app instead of cutting out all the flashcards, you can also study digitally! Find out how to get access here:

This is how you get access:

Below you will find a QR code and a link. Scan the code or type in the link. Then enter your e-mail address so that your Quizlet access can be sent to you.

If you have already installed the Quizlet app, you will be forwarded directly. If you don't have an account yet, you will find an explanation in the confirmation email of exactly how you need to proceed to get free access to the Quizlet app:

www.self-taught-languages.com/the-russian-workbook/

If you have problems getting access, you can always contact me by e-mail and I will give you manual approval for the app:

russian@self-taught-languages.com

Russian	Transliteration	Pronunciation Example
A a	A	"A" as in "car"
Б б	B	"B" as in "bat"
В в	V	"V" as in "van"
Г г	G	"G" as in "go"
Д д	D	"D" as in "dog"
Е е	E	"Ye" as in "yes"
Ё ё	Yo	"Yo" as in "yawn"
Ж ж	Zh	"Zh" as in "treasure" or "pleasure"
З з	Z	"Z" as in "zebra"
И и	I	"Ee" as in "see"
Й й	Y	"Y" as in "boy"
К к	K	"K" as in "kite"
Л л	L	"L" as in "lamp"
М м	M	"M" as in "man"
Н н	N	"N" as in "net"
О о	O	"O" as in "more" (stressed), or "A" as in "car" (unstressed)
П п	P	"P" as in "pen"

Russian	Transliteration	Pronunciation Example
Р р	R	Rolled "R" as in **r**ock (but more rolled)
С с	S	"S" as in "**s**un"
Т т	T	"T" as in "**t**op"
У у	U	"Oo" as in "m**oo**n"
Ф ф	F	"F" as in "**f**un"
Х х	Kh	"H" as in the Scottish "lo**ch**"
Ц ц	Ts	"Ts" as in "ca**ts**"
Ч ч	Ch	"Ch" as in "**ch**at"
Ш ш	Sh	"Sh" as in "**sh**op"
Щ щ	Shch	Softer "Shch," like in "fre**sh ch**eese"
Ъ ъ	Hard sign	No sound; separates hard syllables
Ы ы	Y	A deep "i," as in "**i**ll," but darker
Ь ь	Soft sign	No sound; softens the preceding letter
Э э	E	"E" as in "m**et**"
Ю ю	Yu	"Yu" as in "**u**niverse"
Я я	Ya	"Ya" as in "**ya**rd"

① Info:
The stroke of the capital A can
also be curved like a loop, or
drawn at the end of the word.
Similar to a dot on the i.

Name of Letter: [a]
like **a** in f**a**r

$\mathcal{A}$ $\mathcal{A}$ $\mathcal{A}$ $\mathcal{A}$ $\mathcal{A}$ $\mathcal{A}$ $\mathcal{A}$ $\mathcal{A}$ $\mathcal{A}$ $\mathcal{A}$ $\mathcal{A}$ $\mathcal{A}$

$\mathcal{A}$ $\mathcal{A}$ $\mathcal{A}$ $\mathcal{A}$ $\mathcal{A}$ $\mathcal{A}$ $\mathcal{A}$ $\mathcal{A}$

$\mathcal{A}$ $\mathcal{A}$ $\mathcal{A}$ $\mathcal{A}$

a a a a a a a a a a a a

a a a a a a a a

a a a a

авто [avto]

car

Aa Aa Aa Aa Aa Aa Aa

Aa Aa Aa Aa

Aa Aa

Aaaa Aaaa Aaaa Aaaa

Aaaa Aaaa

Aaaa

💡 Recommendation:
Many people draw the top line at Б last. I recommend drawing it first, as in the example on the left, so that you can continue writing smoothly afterwards.

Б б

Name of Letter: [be]

like b in box

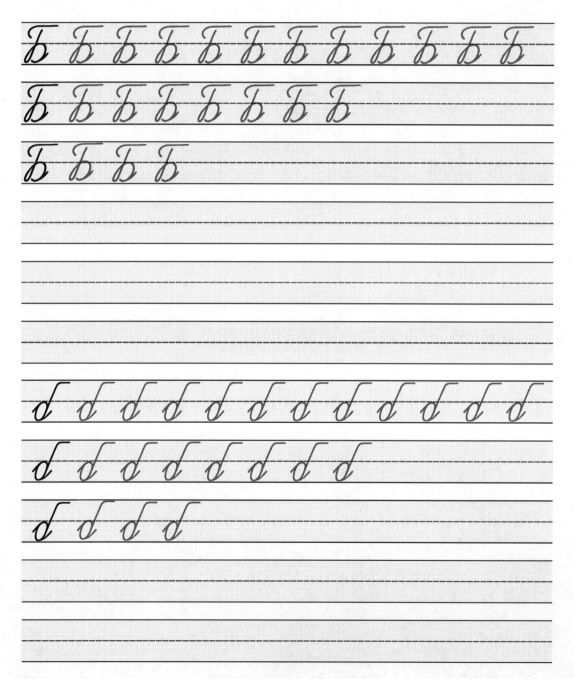

бабушка [babushka]

grandmother

Бб Бб Бб Бб Бб Бб Бб

Бб Бб Бб Бб

Бб Бб

Бдад Бдад Бдад Бдад

Бдад

Бадда Бадда Бадда Бадда

Бадда

ⓘ Info:
The Russian "B" [we] can be written like our "B". But make sure that it is pronounced [we]!

B b

Name of Letter: [ve]
like **v** in **v**oice

𝓑 𝓑 𝓑 𝓑 𝓑 𝓑 𝓑 𝓑 𝓑 𝓑 𝓑 𝓑

𝓑 𝓑 𝓑 𝓑 𝓑 𝓑 𝓑 𝓑

𝓑 𝓑 𝓑 𝓑

𝓫 𝓫 𝓫 𝓫 𝓫 𝓫 𝓫 𝓫 𝓫 𝓫 𝓫 𝓫

𝓫 𝓫 𝓫 𝓫 𝓫 𝓫 𝓫

𝓫 𝓫 𝓫 𝓫

ВИНО [vino]

wine

Вв Вв Вв Вв Вв Вв Вв

Вв Вв Вв Вв

Вв Вв

Ввад Ввад Ввад Ввад

Ввад

Вавдв Вавдв Вавдв Вавдв

Вавдв

Name of Letter: [ge]
like **g** in **g**o

16

голова [golova]

head

Г Г Г Г Г Г Г Г Г Г

Г Г Г Г Г

Глад Глад Глад Глад

Глад

Голыд Голыд Голыд Голыд

Голыд

Голова Голова Голова Голова Голова

Голова

ⓘ Info:

You can write "Д" like our "D" and "д" like the lowercase "g"

Д д

Name of Letter: [de]

like d in day

𝒟 𝒟 𝒟 𝒟 𝒟 𝒟 𝒟 𝒟 𝒟 𝒟 𝒟 𝒟

𝒟 𝒟 𝒟 𝒟 𝒟 𝒟 𝒟 𝒟

𝒟 𝒟 𝒟 𝒟

𝑔 𝑔 𝑔 𝑔 𝑔 𝑔 𝑔 𝑔 𝑔 𝑔 𝑔 𝑔

𝑔 𝑔 𝑔 𝑔 𝑔 𝑔 𝑔 𝑔

𝑔 𝑔 𝑔 𝑔

ДОМ [dom]

house

Dg Dg Dg Dg Dg Dg Dg Dg Dg Dg

Dg Dg Dg Dg Dg Dg

Dad Dad Dad Dad Dad

Dad

Двад Двад Двад Двад

Двад

Дддв Дддв Дддв Дддв Дддв

Дддв

Word exercise with the first 5 letters

There are almost no words that only consist of the first 5 letters.
Nevertheless, here are a few examples for practicing:

[baba]
Older woman

dada dada dada dada

dada dada

dada

[dada]
Childish "yes"

gaga gaga gaga

gaga gaga

gaga

bara bara bara bara

bara bara

bara

dar dar dar dar

dar dar

dar

ⓘ Info:

At the beginning of words, after vowels and after ъ and ь, it is pronounced [ye], like "yet". Before consonants and at the end of words, it is pronounced [e], like "exit".

E e

Name of Letter: [ye]
like **ye** in **ye**t or **e** in **e**xit

Ɛ Ɛ Ɛ Ɛ Ɛ Ɛ Ɛ Ɛ Ɛ Ɛ Ɛ

Ɛ Ɛ Ɛ Ɛ Ɛ Ɛ Ɛ

Ɛ Ɛ Ɛ Ɛ

e e e e e e e e e e e e

e e e e e e e e

e e e e

еда [yeda]

food

Ее Ее Ее Ее Ее Ее Ее Ее Ее Ее Ее Ее Ее

Ее Ее Ее Ее Ее Ее Ее

Ее Ее Ее

еда еда еда еда еда еда еда

еда

елае елае елае елае елае елае

елае

ⓘ Info:

After ж, ч, ш, щ it is pronounced [o], as in "**o**cean". Generally, however, it is pronounced [yo], as in "**yo**ur".

Ё ё

Name of Letter: [yo]
like **yo** in **yo**ur

Ё Ё Ё Ё Ё Ё Ё Ё Ё Ё Ё Ё

Ё Ё Ё Ё Ё Ё Ё Ё

Ё Ё Ё Ё

ё ё ё ё ё ё ё ё ё ё ё ё

ё ё ё ё ё ё ё ё

ё ё ё ё

ёлка [yolka]

christmas tree / fir tree

Ёё Ёё Ёё Ёё Ёё Ёё Ёё Ёё Ёё Ёё Ёё Ёё

Ёё Ёё Ёё Ёё Ёё Ёё Ёё

Ёё Ёё Ёё

ёёа ёёа ёёа ёёа ёёа ёёа ёёа

ёёа

дёда дёда дёда дёда дёда

дёда

жена [zhena]

wife

Жж Жж Жж Жж Жж

Жж Жж Жж

Жж Жж

жёж   жёж   жёж

жёж

З з

Name of Letter: [ze]
like **z** in **z**oo

З З З З З З З З З З З З З

З З З З З З З

З З З

З З З З З З З З З З З З

З З З З З З З

З З З З

зебра [zebra]

zebra

$Зz$ $Зz$ $Зz$ $Зz$ $Зz$ $Зz$ $Зz$ $Зz$ $Зz$

$Зz$ $Зz$ $Зz$ $Зz$ $Зz$ $Зz$

$Зz$ $Зz$ $Зz$

zebza *zebza* *zebza* *zebza* *zebza*

zebza

ⓘ Info:

Although "И" looks like an upside-down "N", it has nothing to do with it. It is pronounced [ee], like in m**ee**t and is written similarly to our "U".

Name of Letter: [i]
like ee in mee**t**

Ии Ии Ии Ии Ии Ии Ии Ии Ии Ии Ии Ии Ии Ии Ии Ии

Ии Ии Ии Ии Ии Ии Ии Ии

Ии Ии Ии

и и и и и и и и и и и и и и и и

и и и и и и и и

и и и и

игра [igra]

game

Ици Ици Ици Ици Ици Ици Ици Ици Ици

Ици Ици Ици Ици Ици Ици

Ици Ици Ици

изба изба изба изба изба

изба

Word exercise with the first 10 letters

ведро ведро ведро ведро   [vedro]
bucket

ведро ведро

ведро

газ газ газ газ газ газ   [gaz]
gas

газ газ

газ

еда еда еда еда еда еда

[yeda]
food

еда еда

еда

жаба жаба жаба

[zhaba]
toad

жаба жаба

жаба

Name of Letter: [y]
like **y** in bo**y**

Й Й Й Й Й Й Й Й Й Й Й Й Й Й Й Й Й

Й Й Й Й Й Й Й Й

Й Й Й

й й й й й й й й й й й й й й й й

й й й й й й й й

й й й й

йога [yoga]

yoga

Йй Йй Йй Йй Йй Йй Йй Йй Йй

Йй Йй Йй Йй Йй Йй

Йй Йй Йй

Йдайz Йдайz Йдайz Йдайz

Йдайz

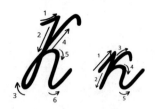

ⓘ Info:

The Russian "K" [ka] is like our "K" [ka] and you can write and pronounce it similarly.

K k

Name of Letter: [ka]

like **k** in **k**ey or **c** in **c**at

К К К К К К К К К К К К К К К

К К К К К К К

К К К

К К К К К К К К К К К К К К К

К К К К К К К К

К К К К

36

кабак [kabak]

pub

Кк Кк Кк Кк Кк Кк Кк Кк Кк

Кк Кк Кк Кк Кк Кк

Кк Кк Кк

кабак кабак кабак кабак

кабак

Л л

Name of Letter: [el]
like **ll** in a**ll**

Лл Лл Лл Лл Лл Лл Лл Лл Лл Лл Лл Лл Лл Лл

Лл Лл Лл Лл Лл Лл Лл

Лл Лл Лл

Лл Лл Лл Лл Лл Лл Лл Лл Лл Лл Лл Лл Лл Лл Лл

Лл Лл Лл Лл Лл Лл Лл Лл

Лл Лл Лл Лл

лад [lad]

harmony

Лл Лл Лл Лл Лл Лл Лл Лл

Лл Лл Лл Лл Лл

Лл Лл Лл

лад лад лад лад лад

лад

Лклэж Лклэж Лклэж

Лклэж

M м

Name of Letter: [em]
like **m** in **man**

$\mathcal{M}$ $\mathcal{M}$ $\mathcal{M}$ $\mathcal{M}$ $\mathcal{M}$ $\mathcal{M}$ $\mathcal{M}$ $\mathcal{M}$

$\mathcal{M}$ $\mathcal{M}$ $\mathcal{M}$ $\mathcal{M}$ $\mathcal{M}$

$\mathcal{M}$ $\mathcal{M}$ $\mathcal{M}$

$\mathcal{M}$ $\mathcal{M}$ $\mathcal{M}$ $\mathcal{M}$ $\mathcal{M}$ $\mathcal{M}$ $\mathcal{M}$ $\mathcal{M}$ $\mathcal{M}$ $\mathcal{M}$

$\mathcal{M}$ $\mathcal{M}$ $\mathcal{M}$ $\mathcal{M}$ $\mathcal{M}$ $\mathcal{M}$ $\mathcal{M}$

$\mathcal{M}$ $\mathcal{M}$ $\mathcal{M}$

кабак [kabak]

pub

Кк Кк Кк Кк Кк Кк Кк Кк Кк

Кк Кк Кк Кк Кк Кк

Кк Кк Кк

кабак кабак кабак кабак

кабак

Л л

Name of Letter: [el]
like **ll** in a**ll**

Л Л Л Л Л Л Л Л Л Л Л Л Л Л

Л Л Л Л Л Л Л

Л Л Л

л л л л л л л л л л л л л л л

л л л л л л л л

л л л л

лад [lad]

harmony

Ллл Ллл Ллл Ллл Ллл Ллл Ллл Ллл

Ллл Ллл Ллл Ллл Ллл

Ллл Ллл Ллл

лад лад лад лад лад

лад

Лклэж Лклэж Лклэж

Лклэж

M м

Name of Letter: [em]
like **m** in **man**

ℳ ℳ ℳ ℳ ℳ ℳ ℳ ℳ

ℳ ℳ ℳ ℳ ℳ

ℳ ℳ ℳ

ɯ ɯ ɯ ɯ ɯ ɯ ɯ ɯ ɯ ɯ ɯ

ɯ ɯ ɯ ɯ ɯ ɯ

ɯ ɯ ɯ

маг [mag]

magician

Мм Мм Мм Мм Мм Мм

Мм Мм Мм Мм

Мм Мм

маг маг маг маг маг

маг

Майкл Майкл Майкл

Майкл

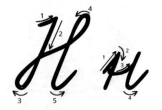

(i) Info:

The capital "H" [n] looks like our "H" [ha], but has nothing to do with it. However, it can be written the same way. The lowercase "н" is written like the capital letter, but in a smaller size. You can write it with (exactly the same as the capital letter) or without loops (see template).

Aussprache: [en]
like **n** in **n**ote

$\mathcal{H}$ $\mathcal{H}$ $\mathcal{H}$ $\mathcal{H}$ $\mathcal{H}$ $\mathcal{H}$ $\mathcal{H}$ $\mathcal{H}$

$\mathcal{H}$ $\mathcal{H}$ $\mathcal{H}$ $\mathcal{H}$ $\mathcal{H}$

$\mathcal{H}$ $\mathcal{H}$ $\mathcal{H}$

$\mathcal{H}$ $\mathcal{H}$ $\mathcal{H}$ $\mathcal{H}$ $\mathcal{H}$ $\mathcal{H}$ $\mathcal{H}$ $\mathcal{H}$ $\mathcal{H}$ $\mathcal{H}$

$\mathcal{H}$ $\mathcal{H}$ $\mathcal{H}$ $\mathcal{H}$ $\mathcal{H}$ $\mathcal{H}$

$\mathcal{H}$ $\mathcal{H}$ $\mathcal{H}$

нива [niva]

field, acre

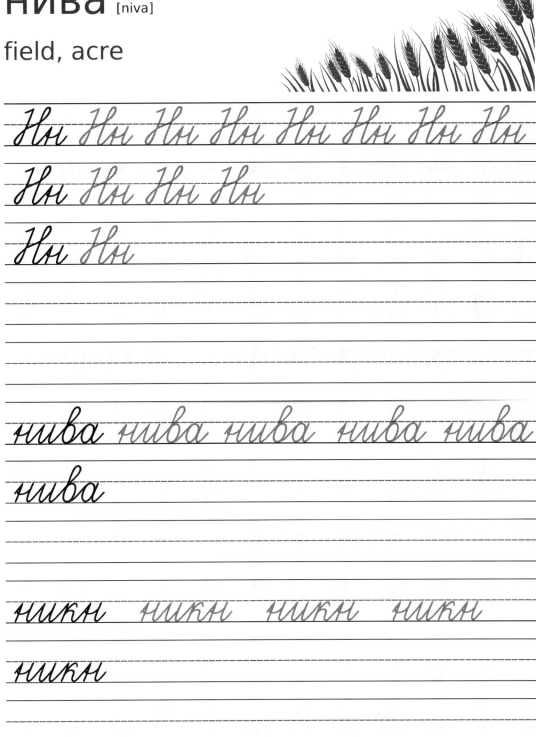

Word exercise with the first 15 letters

белка   белка   белка [belka]
squirrel

белка   белка

вожжи   вожжи   вожжи [vozhzhi]
reins

вожжи   вожжи

глина   глина   глина [glina]
clay, loam

глина   глина

джем джем джем

джем джем

йод йод йод йод йод

йод йод

банк банк банк банк

банк банк

ⓘ Info:

You can write the Russian "O" exactly like our "O", both the lowercase and the uppercase.

O o

Name of Letter: [o]
like o in n**o**t

O O O O O O O O O O O O

O O O O O O

O O O

o o o o o o o o o o o o o

o o o o o o o

o o o

46

ОКНО [okno]

window

Oo Oo Oo Oo Oo Oo Oo Oo

Oo Oo Oo Oo

Oo Oo

онво онво онво онво онво

онво

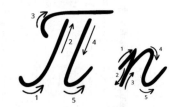

П П П П П П П П П П П

П П П П П П

П П П

п п п п п п п п п п п

п п п п п п п

п п п

папа [papa]

dad, father

Пп Пп Пп Пп Пп Пп Пп

Пп Пп Пп Пп

Пп Пп

папа папа папа папа

папа

(i) Info:

The Russian "P" [er] is very similar to our "P" [pe], but has nothing to do with it. The lowercase "p" [er] is also usually written slightly differently than we would write the lowercase "p" [pe].

P p

Name of Letter: [er]
like **r** in **r**ock
(but rolled)

𝒫 𝒫 𝒫 𝒫 𝒫 𝒫 𝒫 𝒫 𝒫 𝒫 𝒫 𝒫

𝒫 𝒫 𝒫 𝒫 𝒫 𝒫

𝒫 𝒫 𝒫

𝓅 𝓅 𝓅 𝓅 𝓅 𝓅 𝓅 𝓅 𝓅 𝓅 𝓅 𝓅

𝓅 𝓅 𝓅 𝓅 𝓅 𝓅 𝓅

𝓅 𝓅 𝓅

радио [radio]

radio

Рр Рр Рр Рр Рр Рр Рр Рр Рр

Рр Рр Рр Рр Рр

Рр Рр

радио радио радио радио

радио

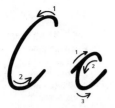

ⓘ Info:

The Russian "C" [es] is very similar to our "C", but has nothing to do with it. However, it can be written the same way in upper and lower case.

C c

Name of Letter: [es]
like **s** in **s**un

C C C C C C C C C C C

C C C C C C

C C C

C C C C C C C C C C C C

C C C C C C

C C C

сила [sila]

power / strength

Сс Сс Сс Сс Сс Сс Сс Сс Сс Сс

Сс Сс Сс Сс Сс

Сс Сс

сила сила сила сила

сила

☀ Recommendation:
For the capital "T" [te], I recommend drawing the upper stroke after the middle one so that you can continue writing smoothly. The small "т" is written like our "m".

T т

Name of Letter: [te]
like **t** in **t**able

𝒯𝒯 𝒯𝒯 𝒯𝒯 𝒯𝒯 𝒯𝒯 𝒯𝒯 𝒯𝒯 𝒯𝒯 𝒯𝒯

𝒯𝒯 𝒯𝒯 𝒯𝒯 𝒯𝒯 𝒯𝒯

𝒯𝒯 𝒯𝒯 𝒯𝒯

m m m m m m m m m m

m m m m m m

m m m

топор [topor]

axe

Ттm Ттm Ттm Ттm Ттm Ттm

Ттm Ттm Ттm Ттm

Ттm Ттm

топор   топор   топор

топор

Word exercise with the first 20 letters

год год год год год

[God]
year

год год

бартер бартер

[Barter]
barter trade

бартер бартер

клоп клоп клоп клоп

[Klop]
bug

клоп клоп

минор минор минор minor (music)

минор минор

свет свет свет свет свет light

свет свет

жир жир жир жир fat

жир жир

ⓘ Info:

The capital and lowercase Russian "У" [oo] is very similar to our lowercase "y". The capital "У" [oo] is written like our lowercase "y", only without the loop and capitalized.

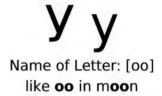

Name of Letter: [oo]

like **oo** in m**oo**n

Y Y Y Y Y Y Y Y Y Y Y Y

Y Y Y Y Y

Y Y Y

у у у у у у у у у у у у у у

у у у у у у у

у у у

урок [oorok]

lesson

Уу Уу Уу Уу Уу Уу Уу Уу Уу

Уу Уу Уу Уу Уу

Уу Уу Уу

урок урок урок урок урок

урок

ⓘ Info:
Probably the most difficult letter. There are several ways to write it beautifully. This is just one of many possibilities

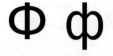

Name of Letter: [ef]

like f in food

60

флаг [flag]

flag

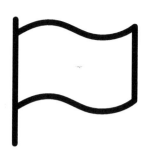

Фф Фф Фф Фф Фф Фф Фф Фф Фф

Фф Фф Фф Фф Фф

Фф Фф Фф

флаг флаг флаг флаг флаг

флаг

☀ Recommendation:
Even though "X" [kha] looks like
our "X", in handwriting it is
written more like two "Cs" that
mirror each other

Name of Letter: [kha]

like **ch** in Scottish lo**ch**

𝒳 𝒳 𝒳 𝒳 𝒳 𝒳 𝒳 𝒳 𝒳 𝒳

𝒳 𝒳 𝒳 𝒳 𝒳

𝒳 𝒳 𝒳

𝓍 𝓍 𝓍 𝓍 𝓍 𝓍 𝓍 𝓍 𝓍 𝓍 𝓍 𝓍 𝓍

𝓍 𝓍 𝓍 𝓍 𝓍 𝓍 𝓍

𝓍 𝓍 𝓍

храм [khram]

temple or church

Xx Xx Xx Xx Xx Xx Xx

Xx Xx Xx Xx Xx

Xx Xx Xx

храм храм храм храм

храм

☼ Recommendation:
You can write the Russian "Ц" [tsch] like our "U", followed by a very small "j" without a dot.

Name of Letter: [tse]
like **ts** in boo**ts**

Ц Ц Ц Ц Ц Ц Ц Ц Ц Ц

Ц Ц Ц Ц Ц

Ц Ц Ц

Цу Цу Цу Цу Цу Цу Цу Цу Цу Цу Цу Цу Цу

Цу Цу Цу Цу Цу Цу Цу

Цу Цу Цу

цех [tsekh]

workshop

Цц Цц Цц Цц Цц Цц Цц Цц

Цц Цц Цц Цц Цц

Цц Цц Цц

цех цех цех цех цех

цех

Ч ч

Name of Letter: [che]
like **ch** in **ch**at

Ч Ч Ч Ч Ч Ч Ч Ч Ч Ч Ч Ч Ч Ч

Ч Ч Ч Ч Ч Ч Ч

Ч Ч Ч

ч ч ч ч ч ч ч ч ч ч ч ч ч ч

ч ч ч ч ч ч ч

ч ч ч

череп [tscherep]

skull

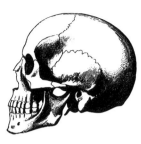

Чч Чч Чч Чч Чч Чч Чч Чч Чч Чч

Чч Чч Чч Чч Чч Чч

Чч Чч Чч

череп череп череп череп

череп

Word exercise with the first 25 letters

мост мост мост мост   [Most]
                                                      bridge

мост мост

балет балет балет   [Ballet]
                                                    ballet

балет балет

книга книга книга книга   [Kniga]
                                                    book

книга книга

лодка лодка лодка boat

лодка лодка

весло весло весло весло rudder

весло весло

привет привет привет hello

привет привет

(i) Info:

"Ш" [sha] is somewhat similar to our "W" in both upper and lower case, but has nothing to do with it.

Name of Letter: [sha]
like **sh** in **sh**ort

Ш Ш Ш Ш Ш Ш Ш Ш Ш Ш Ш Ш

Ш Ш Ш Ш Ш Ш Ш

Ш Ш Ш

ш ш ш ш ш ш ш ш ш ш ш ш

ш ш ш ш ш ш ш

ш ш ш

шина [shina]

tires

Шин Шин Шин Шин Шин Шин Шин

Шин Шин Шин Шин

Шин Шин

шина шина шина шина

шина

☼ Recommendation:
"Щ" [shcha] is written like
"Ш" [sha] plus the small "j"
at the end of "Ц" [tse]

Aussprache: [shcha]
like **sh_ch** in
fre**sh_ch**eese

Щ Щ Щ Щ Щ Щ Щ Щ Щ Щ Щ

Щ Щ Щ Щ Щ Щ Щ

Щ Щ Щ

Щ Щ Щ Щ Щ Щ Щ Щ Щ Щ Щ

Щ Щ Щ Щ Щ Щ Щ

Щ Щ Щ

щука [shchuka]

pike (fish)

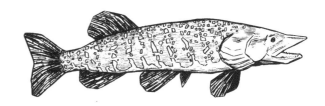

Щщщ Щщщ Щщщ Щщщ Щщщ Щщщ

Щщщ Щщщ Щщщ Щщщ

Щщщ Щщщ

щука щука щука щука

щука

Hardness and
softness signs

Ъ Ы Ь

(i) Info:

ъ is not pronounced and can only be placed between a consonant and the vowels -е, -ё, -ю, -я. The consonant is hard and the following vowels -е, -ё, -ю, -я are pronounced with j (je, jo, ju, ja).

ъ

hard sign
has no sound

ъ   ъ   ъ   ъ   ъ   ъ   ъ   ъ   ъ   ъ

ъ   ъ   ъ   ъ   ъ   ъ

ъ   ъ   ъ

объект   объект   объект

[Ob'yekt]
Objekt

объект   объект

Ы

ⓘ Info:

"ы" [i] can be written like a small "B" and a small "L". Pronounced after hard consonants (except ш and ж) like **i** in **i**ll.

ы ы ы ы ы ы ы ы ы ы ы ы

ы ы ы ы ы ы

ы ы ы

[Pyl']
Staub

пыль пыль пыль пыль

пыль пыль

76

(i) Info:

ь wird nicht ausgesprochen. Der vorhergegangene Konsonant ist weich und die nachfolgenden Vokale -e, -ё, -и, -ю, -я werden mit j ausgesprochen (je, jo, ji, ju, ja).

ь

soft sign
has no sound

ь *ь* *ь* *ь* *ь* *ь* *ь* *ь* *ь* *ь* *ь*

ь *ь* *ь* *ь* *ь* *ь* *ь*

ь *ь* *ь*

[Noch']
Nacht

ночь *ночь* *ночь* *ночь*

ночь *ночь*

77

It is important to make the stroke in the middle after the large arc so that it is not confused with "3" [ze].

Э э

Name of Letter: [e]

like **e** in **e**nd

Э Э Э Э Э Э Э Э Э Э Э Э Э Э

Э Э Э Э Э Э Э

Э Э Э

Э Э Э Э Э Э Э Э Э Э Э Э Э

Э Э Э Э Э Э Э Э

Э Э Э

экран [ekrán]

screen

Ээ Ээ Ээ Ээ Ээ Ээ Ээ Ээ Ээ

Ээ Ээ Ээ Ээ Ээ Ээ

Ээ Ээ Ээ

экран экран экран экран

экран

Ю ю

Aussprache: [yoo]

like **u** in **u**se

Ю Ю Ю Ю Ю Ю Ю Ю Ю Ю Ю

Ю Ю Ю Ю Ю Ю Ю

Ю Ю Ю

ю ю ю ю ю ю ю ю ю ю ю ю ю

ю ю ю ю ю ю ю ю

ю ю ю

юбка [yubka]

skirt

Юю Юю Юю Юю Юю Юю Юю

Юю Юю Юю Юю Юю

Юю Юю

юбка юбка юбка юбка

юбка

ⓘ Info:
Although "Я" [ya] looks like a
mirrored "R", the two have
nothing to do with each other.

Я я

Name of Letter: [ya]
like ya in yard

Я Я Я Я Я Я Я Я Я Я Я

Я Я Я Я Я Я Я Я

Я Я Я

Я Я Я Я Я Я Я Я Я Я Я Я Я Я

Я Я Я Я Я Я Я Я

Я Я Я

яблоко [yabloko]

apple

Яя Яя Яя Яя Яя Яя Яя Яя

Яя Яя Яя Яя Яя

Яя Яя

яблоко яблоко яблоко

яблоко

Words and simple sentences
слова и простые предложения

Congratulations! You have now learned all the letters. On the following pages you will find lots more word and sentence exercises to help you refine what you have learned.

Important: When writing the words, always say the word as it is pronounced in your head or out loud. That's why the pronunciation is always on the right. This way you really associate the characters with their meaning and don't just learn to write them. For a really 100% correct pronunciation, I recommend that you have the word read aloud by a translator (Google Translate or similar).

This is followed by 20 pages of templates for flash cards. You can cut out individual squares and then have flash cards with which you can learn the 100 most important Russian words. This book will give you a solid foundation to continue learning Russian.

[zdrastvooytye]
hello

здравствуйте

здравствуйте

[yavlenie]
phenomenon

явление   явление

явление   явление

[rooskiy]
russian

русский русский

русский русский

правительство

[pruhveetel'stvuh]
government

правительство

правительство

лифт лифт лифт

[lift]
elevator

лифт лифт

прогулка

[progoolka]
walk

прогулка Прогулка

продукты питания [prodookty peetaneeya]
food products

продукты питания

инструмент [eenstrumyent]
instrument

инструмент

гигиена гигиена [geegiyena]
hygiene

гигиена гигиена

Привет, меня зовут

Привет, меня зовут

Я бы хотела яблоко

Я бы хотела яблоко

Я говорю по-русски

Я говорю по-русски

Я из Германии

Я из Германии

[ya ees gyermanee]
I'm from Germany

Одну воду, пожалуйста

Одну воду, пожалуйста.

[odnoo vdoo pazhaloosta]
Just one water, please

Как вас зовут?

Как вас зовут?

[kak vas zovoot]
What is your name?

[izvineetye]
Sorry

извините

извините Извините

[gdyeh nakhahdeetsah tooalyet]
Where is the restroom

Где находится туалет

Где находится туалет

[katoryj chas]
What time is it?

Который час?

Который час?

железнодорожный вокзал **railway station**

железнодорожный вокзал

Вон тот дом белый. That house over there is white.

Вон тот дом белый.

Мне 30 лет **I'm 30 years old**

Мне 30 лет

Я люблю есть торт [ya lyublyu yest' tort]
I like to eat cake

Я люблю есть торт

Как я выгляжу? [kak ya vyglyazhu]
How do I look?

Как я выгляжу?

Сейчас четверть шестого. [seychas chelvyert' shyestova]
It's a quarter to six.

Сейчас четверть шестого.

Железнодорожный вокзал

Железнодорожный вокзал

[von tot dom belyj]
That house over there is white.

Вон тот дом белый.

Вон тот дом белый.

[mnye trid-tsat' lyet]
I'm 30 years old

Мне 30 лет

Мне 30 лет

Flashcards to cut
out & practice

флэш-карты

Also available digitally via Quizlet:

Simply scan with your smartphone.
Learn from anywhere at any time with the app.

да [da]	нет [nyet]
здравствуйте [zdravstvuyte]	спасибо [spasibo]
извините [izvinite]	пожалуйста [pozhaluysta]
как дела? [kak dye-la]	хорошо [khorosho]
что? [chto?]	плохо [plokho]

no	yes
thanks	hello
please	Sorry
good	How is it going?
bad	What?

где? [gde?]	когда? [kogda?]
почему? [pochemu?]	кто? [kto?]
сколько? [skolko?]	вода [voda]
чай [chay]	кофе [kofe]
еда [yeda]	дом [dom]

When?	Where?
Who?	Why?
water	How much?
coffee	tea
house	food

магазин [magazin]	работа [rabota]
школа [shkola]	больница [bol'nitsa]
аптека [apteka]	парк [park]
ресторан [restoran]	гостиница [gostinitsa]
туалет [tualet]	улица [ulica]

work	store

hospital	school

park	drugstore

hotel	restaurant

street	toilet

машина [mashina]	автобус [avtobus]
поезд [poezd]	самолёт [samolet]
время [vremya]	день [den']
утро [utro]	ночь [noch']
вечер [vecher]	неделя [nedelya]

bus	car
airplane	train
day	time
night	morning
week	evening

месяц [mesyats]	год [god]
январь [yanvar']	февраль [fevral']
март [mart]	апрель [aprel']
май [may]	июнь [iyun']
июль [iyul']	август [avgust]

year	month
february	january
april	march
june	may
july	august

сентябрь [sentyabr']	октябрь [oktyabr']
ноябрь [noyabr']	декабрь [dekabr']
цвет [tsvet]	животное [zhivotnoe]
растение [rastenie]	человек [chelovek]
друг [drug]	семья [semya]

october	september
december	november
animal	color
human	plant
family	friend

мать	отец
[mat']	[otec]

брат	сестра
[brat]	[sestra]

ребёнок	любовь
[rebyonok]	[lyubov']

женщина	мужчина
[zhenshchina]	[muzhchina]

деньги	ключ
[den'gi]	[klyuch]

father	mother
sister	brother
love	child
man	woman
key	money

книга [kniga]	телефон [telefon]
карта [karta]	город [gorod]
страна [strana]	море [more]
озеро [ozero]	река [reka]
гора [gora]	лес [les]

phone	book
city	map
sea	country
river	lake
forest	mountain

один [odin]	два [dva]
три [tri]	четыре [chetyre]
пять [pyat']	шесть [shest']
семь [sem']	восемь [vosem']
девять [devyat']	десять [desyat']

2	1
4	3
6	5
8	7
10	9

одиннадцать
[odinnadtsat']

двенадцать
[dvenadtsat']

тринадцать
[trinadtsat']

четырнадцать
[chetyrnadtsat']

пятнадцать
[pyatnadtsat']

шестнадцать
[shestnadtsat']

семнадцать
[semnadtsat']

восемнадцать
[sosemnadtsat']

девятнадцать
[devyatnadtsat']

двадцать
[dvadtsat']

12	11
14	13
16	15
18	17
20	19

© 2024 Self-taught Russian

russian@self-taught-languages.com

Autor:
Nikita Kuznetsov
& Andrey Bernhart

Publisher:
Buchblick Verlag
represented by
Andrey Bernhart
Bahnhofstraße 17
6824 Schlins
Austria
office@buchblickverlag.com

ISBN:
9798323784097

Made in the USA
Las Vegas, NV
19 December 2024

14786963R00066